HOTBEDS
AND
COLDFRAMES

THE CLASSIC USDA FARMERS' BULLETIN NO. 1743
WITH TIPS AND TRADITIONAL METHODS
IN SUSTAINABLE VEGETABLE GARDENING AND PLANT
PROPAGATION IN SMALL GREENHOUSES

BY **U.S. DEPARTMENT OF AGRICULTURE**

ORIGINALLY PUBLISHED IN 1935

Legacy Edition
CLASSIC FARMERS BULLETIN LIBRARY
BOOK NO. 1743

Doublebit Press
Eugene, OR

New content, introduction, and annotations
Copyright © 2020 by Doublebit Press. All rights reserved.

Doublebit Press is an imprint of Eagle Nest Press
www.doublebitpress.com | Eugene, OR, USA

Original content under the public domain. Originally published in 1935 by the U.S. Department of Agriculture.

This title, along with other Doublebit Press books including the Classic Farmers Bulletin Library, are available at a volume discount for youth groups, outdoors clubs, or reading groups.

Doublebit Press Legacy Edition ISBN
Paperback: 978-1-64389-147-7

Disclaimer: Because of its age and historic context, this book could contain content on present-day inappropriate methods, activities, outdated medical information, unsafe chemical and mechanical processes, or culturally and racially insensitive content. Doublebit Press, or its employees, authors, and other affiliates, assume no liability for any actions performed by readers or any damages that might be related to information contained in this book. This text has been published for historical study and for personal literary enrichment toward the goal of preserving the American handcraft tradition, timeless trade skills, and traditional artisanal knowledge.

First Doublebit Press Legacy Edition Printing, 2020

Printed in the United States of America when purchased at retail in the USA

INTRODUCTION
Classic Farmers Bulletin Library

The old experts of artisanal trades, country and homestead knowledge, and the woods and mountains taught timeless principles and skills for centuries. Through their timeless books, the old experts offered rich descriptions of how the world works and encouraged learning through personal experiences *by doing*. Over the last 125 years, manufacturing, farming, and construction have substantially changed. Of course, many things have gotten simpler as equipment and technology have improved. In addition, some activities of pre-digital times are now no longer in vogue, or are even outright considered inappropriate or illegal. However, despite many of the positive changes in manufacturing and crafting methods that have occurred over the years, *there are many other skills and much knowledge that have been forgotten.*

By publishing the reprint series of the old USDA *Farmers' Bulletin*, it is our goal at Doublebit Press to do what we can to preserve and share the works from forgotten teachers that form the cornerstone of the history of the American artisans and traditional crafts. So much farm, homestead, and handcraft knowledge was passed to each generation through experience and hard work. An original mission of the US Department of Agriculture was to optimize farm outputs and increase the quality of life on farms through handcrafts, construction, and old-time farm tricks, tips, and skills. In their *Farmers' Bulletin* series, the USDA captured and passed on knowledge that applied to far more than just farmers!

Through remastered reprint editions of timeless classics, perhaps we can regain some of this lost knowledge for future generations. Today's interest in mastery of old handcraft skills, homestead self-sufficiency, and artisanal character has renewed an interest in the old arts. Luckily, the USDA's *Farmers' Bulletin* series contains thousands of pamphlets dedicated to teaching, improving life, and ensuring self-sufficiency to thrive in both the city and on a farm.

This book is an important contribution traditional handcraft and country skills literature and has important historical and collector value toward preserving the American handcraft and outdoors tradition. The knowledge it holds is an invaluable reference for practicing skills and hand craft methods. Its chapters thoroughly discuss some of the essential building blocks of knowledge that are fundamental but may have been forgotten as equipment gets fancier and technology gets smarter. In short, this reprint of the *Farmers' Bulletin* pamphlets was chosen for Legacy Edition printing because much of the basic skills and knowledge it contains has been forgotten or put to the wayside in trade for more modern conveniences and methods.

With technology playing a major role in everyday life, sometimes we need to take a step back in time to find those basic building blocks used for gaining mastery – the things that we have luckily not completely lost and has been recorded in books over the last two centuries. These skills aren't forgotten, they've just been shelved. *It's time to unshelve them once again and reclaim the lost knowledge of self-sufficiency.*

Based on this commitment to preserving our outdoors and handcraft artisanal heritage, we have taken great pride in publishing this book as a complete original work. We hope it is worthy of both study and collection by outdoors folk in the modern era of outdoors and traditional skills life.

Unlike many other photocopy reproductions of classic books that are common on the market, this Legacy Edition does not simply place poor photography of old texts on our pages and use error-prone optical scanning or computer-generated text. We want our work to speak for itself, and reflect the quality demanded by our customers who spend their hard-earned money. With this in mind, each Legacy Edition book that has been chosen for publication is carefully remastered from original print books, *with the Doublebit Legacy Edition printed and laid out in the exact way that it was presented at its original publication.* We provide a beautiful, memorable experience that is as true to the original text as best as possible, but with the aid of modern technology to make as beautiful a reading experience as possible for books that can be over a century old.

Because of its age and because it is presented in its original form, the book may contain misspellings, inking errors from print plates, and other printing blemishes that were common for the age. However, these are exactly the things that we feel give the book its character, which we preserved in this Legacy Edition. During digitization, we ensured that each illustration in the text was clean and sharp with the least amount of loss from being copied and digitized as possible. Full-page plate illustrations are presented as they were found, often including the extra blank page that was often behind a plate. For the covers, we use the original cover design to give the book its original feel. We are sure you'll appreciate the fine touches and attention to detail that your Legacy Edition has to offer.

For traditional handcrafters and classic artisanal enthusiasts who demand the best from their equipment, this Doublebit Press Legacy Edition reprint was made with you in mind. Both important and minor details have equally both been accounted for by our publishing staff, down to the cover, font, layout, and images. It is the goal of Doublebit Legacy Edition series to be worthy of collection in any outdoorsperson's library and that can be passed to future generations.

Every book selected to be in this series offers unique views and instruction on important skills, advice, tips, tidbits, anecdotes, stories, and experiences that will enrich the repertoire of any person who enjoys escaping a bit from today's modern technology-based, cookie-cutter, and highly industrialized skills. Instead, folks seeking to make things with their hands like the old days may find great value from these resurrected instructional manuals from the past. These books were not simply written to be shelved in a library – they contain our history and forgotten methods to make things with real character and energy with a *human* component.

Therefore, to learn the most basic building blocks of a craft leads to mastery of all its aspects. We hope this book helps you along this path with its rich descriptions and illustrations!

About the USDA Farmers' Bulletin Series

Back in the early 1900s, the US Department of Agriculture (USDA) began publication of small pamphlets that were meant to improve the outputs of America's farms, promote self-sufficiency, and help farmers and farming communities thrive. This publication series continued for decades, and volumes were always available when someone wanted to learn more about a specific skill or topic that could come in handy on the homestead.

Each of the 2,000+ volumes specializes in one specific topic, be it growing a certain crop, raising a particular animal, or building a type of farm structure. Each of the pamphlets captured the best knowledge available at that time, which often represented decades or centuries of old farmer knowledge, which we know, is incredibly useful and reliable!

As we continue to blaze paths into the digital frontier, many of these lost "farmers' tips" have become more useful than ever, particularly to folks looking to start homesteads and small-scale farms, as well as those who just want to live more sustainably, simply, and consciously in light of today's factory processed world. The *Farmers' Bulletin* is also highly useful for people who live in cities, as they contain much information for community gardens, urban and rooftop farming, and sustainable living tips.

Unfortunately, many of these print volumes of the *Farmers' Bulletin* are now out of print. Indeed, because these texts are in the public domain, they are easily found and are available on the Internet. However, many of these books that are easily found on the web are often low-resolution photocopies, complete with scribble marks or other distracting spots. For the first time, high-quality, professionally restored *Farmers' Bulletin* reissues are being made by Doublebit Press to increase access to the timeless knowledge that each contains.

This Doublebit Press Legacy Edition republishes this tradition of handcrafted quality and artisanal work. We hope that this deluxe printed edition of this book will help you gain mastery in your craft, as it is presented in the exact form that it was originally published. Even today, the knowledge contained within its pages are timeless and have much to teach!

Finally, as works of art, the USDA *Farmers' Bulletin* issues contain beautiful illustrations and line art that are a sign of simpler, yet authentic times when quality mattered and craftsmanship was king. This collectible volume makes a great addition to the bookshelf of any handcrafter, maker, artisan, farmer, homesteader, or outdoors enthusiast!

Enjoy some old-time, vintage charm when the government actually encouraged you to be self-sufficient with these beautifully illustrated and classic instruction manuals by the USDA!

HOTBEDS AND COLDFRAMES

FARMERS'
BULLETIN
Nº 1743

U.S. DEPARTMENT OF AGRICULTURE

HOTBEDS AND COLDFRAMES are being used by home and market gardeners for starting early plants, especially in sections of the country where the growing season is short and it is desirable to advance the development of certain crops. Coldframes are being extensively employed for the growing of a number of vegetable crops to a marketable stage, especially in sections along the Atlantic coast where the weather during the fall and spring is mild and only a moderate amount of protection is necessary.

With the present scarcity of horse-stable manure suitable for the heating of hotbeds, growers are turning to other forms of heating, including wood-burning flues, steam, and hot water. Recently, electricity has come into the field of plant-bed heating and has been found practicable under favorable conditions, especially where electric current can be secured at a low rate and where accurate temperature control is desirable.

Conservation of heat is an important factor in the construction and operation of hotbeds and coldframes, and numerous types of mats and coverings for protecting the beds have been devised. The growth of plants in hotbeds is greatly hastened as a result of raising the soil temperature, but care must be taken to control the temperature and to accustom the plants to outdoor conditions before they are set in the open ground.

Many gardeners have constructed small greenhouses and more or less permanent plant-growing structures in which to sow seeds and start early plants, but coldframes are desirable for use in gradually tempering the plants to outdoor conditions.

For the convenience of growers, brief instructions are included in this bulletin for the growing of early plants in the various types of plant-growing structures described.

Washington, D. C.   Issued February 1935
                         Slightly revised August 1941

HOTBEDS AND COLDFRAMES

By W. R. BEATTIE, *senior horticulturist, Division of Fruit and Vegetable Crops and Diseases, Bureau of Plant Industry*

CONTENTS

	Page		Page
Introduction	1	Growing early plants	23
Location of hotbeds and coldframes	3	Tomatoes	23
Manure hotbeds	3	Peppers	24
Fuel-heated beds	8	Eggplants	24
Flue-heated beds	8	Summer squashes	25
Pipe-heated beds	11	Cucumbers	25
Electric heating of beds and plant houses	12	Muskmelons	26
Construction of coldframes	16	Lettuce	26
Coverings for hotbeds and coldframes	16	Cabbage and broccoli	27
Glazed-sash coverings	18	Cauliflower	27
Cloth coverings	20	Celery	27
Substitutes for glass and cloth	21		
Care of hotbeds and coldframes	21		
Ventilation	22		
Watering	22		

INTRODUCTION

EARLINESS is an important factor to both home and market gardeners in the production of such crops as tomatoes, peppers, eggplant, lettuce, and other vegetables that can be readily transplanted. Various forms of plant-growing structures, including greenhouses, sash houses, hotbeds, plant pits, and coldframes, are being used by gardeners for starting early plants, the type of structure or frame used depending largely on climatic and other local conditions. In the past, when an abundance of horse manure was available, the manure-heated hotbed was used almost exclusively, but with the present shortage of horse manure, growers have turned very largely to fuel-heated beds for starting early plants. The tendency is also toward using greenhouses more generally for starting early plants, but continuing the employment of coldframes for tempering the plants to outdoor conditions before setting them in the open.

In determining the type of house or bed to use for starting early plants, the grower must first consider the temperature and other climatic conditions under which he is working. His object is to produce good, stocky, well-built plants that will stand transplanting to the open without serious checking of their growth. Under certain climatic conditions this may require the use of a heated greenhouse. Under other conditions this end can be best attained by the employment of manure- or fuel-heated hotbeds, while in still other cases, where only slight protection is required, a cloth- or sash-covered coldframe may be sufficient. In this bulletin the various types of plant-growing beds are discussed, together with suggestions as to their management and the proper treatment of the various kinds of plants that are commonly grown under protection during the early spring or the late fall.

Hotbeds and coldframes are frequently used in regions with a mild climate, for growing to a marketable stage certain vegetables such as cucumbers, beets, radishes, carrots, parsley, lettuce, and occasionally muskmelons. In some cases sash-covered frames are employed for the early crop, and after it is well started and the danger of injurious temperatures is past, the frames are removed and the crop matured in the open. This is known as frame culture. It is used most extensively by growers along the Atlantic seaboard where the natural heat of the sun during the early spring and late fall is sufficient to maintain a growing temperature. Where this system is used for growing late-fall crops the plants are started in open beds; then as the weather becomes cool the frames are placed in position and the sash or cloth covering put on. The reverse plan is followed in the spring.

Where hotbeds or coldframes are constructed of brick or poured concrete, the walls are usually made 4 inches thick and are carried 20 to 24 inches above normal ground level at the back and 10 to 12 inches above it at the front. The usual width of these beds having such walls is 6 feet from center to center of the walls, or approximately 5 feet 8 inches inside measurement. By making the tops of the walls conform to the slope of the bed, the sash will have 2 inches of a firm supporting surface on top of each wall. Where crosspieces are provided, upon which to slide the sash, they are embedded in the concrete or brickwork and are flush with the top of the walls. If desirable, a wooden housing for the upper end of the sash may be provided and embedded into the wall or fastened with bolts let into the wall.

Concrete and cinder blocks are being used quite extensively for the construction of the walls of hotbeds, coldframes, and small plant houses, on account of the ease with which they can be laid. In some localities concrete blocks 4 inches thick can be obtained, and walls constructed of these occupy less space than those made of the 6- or 8-inch blocks. Where concrete blocks are used for the front and back walls of the beds, it is necessary to put up forms and pour the top of the ends in order to obtain the correct slope. The 8- by 8- by 16-inch concrete and cinder blocks are especially adapted for constructing the walls of double beds with a ridge through the center and covered by means of two lines of hotbed sash or cloth. The top layer of blocks should be crowned with a layer of cement mortar about an inch in thickness to prevent water from entering the cavities of the blocks. Cinder blocks are better insulators against the passage of heat than concrete and, in addition, have the advantage that nails can be driven into them where wood is being fastened to the block walls.

Double plant beds 12 to 15 feet in width with concrete- or cinder-block walls are coming into more general use for plant growing, on account of low cost of construction. Where flue or hot-water heating is employed the side walls need be only about 16 inches, or two layers of blocks in height, above the ground level. Where sash are used as a covering, a plank is supported on posts through the center of the bed, and the double row of sash rest on this plank at the center and on the walls of the bed at the sides. The slope given the sash is usually from 12 to 18 inches for the full length of the 6-foot sash. If muslin or light canvas is used as a covering, the slope is increased to about 2 feet and side rafters or strips are provided on which the canvas rests.

LOCATION OF HOTBEDS AND COLDFRAMES

Hotbeds and coldframes should always be located on well-drained land that is free from depressions or danger of flooding during heavy rains. A location near the house where the beds can be given frequent attention is desirable. The beds should be protected on the north by a group of buildings, a grove of trees, a tight board fence, or an evergreen hedge. In many cases windbreaks, consisting of pine boughs or bundles of corn fodder set against supports, are employed for protecting the beds from cold winds. The growers around Norfolk and Portsmouth, Va., divide their frame yards into 1-acre sections by means of arborvitae and California privet hedges that attain a height of 12 to 20 feet, and very effectively break the force of the wind. (See cover illustration.) A location with a southern exposure and adequate wind protection on the north and west is ideal. In all cases, protection from cold winds, the securing of direct sunlight, and convenience in the matter of tending should be the main determining factors in the selection of a location for any type of plant bed.

Plant beds and small greenhouses built well below the level of the ground require less heat than those that are entirely above ground and more exposed. This principle applies especially to the construction of sash-covered houses that are heated by flues, stoves, or electricity. Special care must be taken, however, in the selection of a location for beds and houses that are partially below ground, to provide good drainage in order to avoid flooding the beds during rainy seasons.

Plants grown in hotbeds and coldframes require rather frequent watering and, if possible, the beds should be located where water can be piped to them. In some cases a well is dug or drilled near the beds and a pump installed to supply the water. Where the beds are of a very temporary nature, water is sometimes hauled in barrels or tank wagons and applied to the plants by means of sprinkling cans. In any case an adequate supply of water for watering the plants must be provided. In the east-Texas tomato fields several barrels of water are hauled and placed alongside each bed at the beginning of the plant-growing season. In other instances water is hauled in tank wagons or in the tanks of orchard sprayers and is applied to the plant beds through a hose having a rose or sprinkler on its end. The most convenient method of watering the plant beds, however, is by means of water under pressure piped direct to the beds.

MANURE HOTBEDS

Where manure is plentiful, temporary hotbeds may be provided by simply placing a flat pile of manure 8 or 9 feet in width, 12 to 24 inches in depth, and of any desired length, on top of the ground in a well-drained location, and setting frames of boards on top of it to contain the soil and support the covering of sash or cloth. Additional manure is then banked around the outside of the frames to retain heat.

The frames usually consist of 1-inch boards, preferably cypress, redwood, or white pine, 12 inches wide, 1 board being used for the front or south side and 2 boards, 1 above the other, for the back or north side. These boards are nailed to stakes driven through the bed of manure and into the ground, the lines of boards being 5 feet 8 inches apart so that the space between them can be covered with standard 3- by 6-foot hotbed sash that rest on the edges of the boards that form the sides of the bed. Sectional or portable frames with sloping ends to carry 4 or 5 standard sash are often constructed, and where a long bed is required the sections are placed end to end, making a continuous bed.

The preparation and handling of the manure used in making a temporary hotbed of this character are practically the same as those described herein for more permanent beds.

About 5 inches of good soil (or sand if sweetpotato plants are to be grown) should be spread on top of the manure in the frames before the sash is put on. This method of constructing manure-heated beds avoids the necessity of digging a pit but requires about twice the amount of manure. However, this material is usually in good condition for top-dressing land or for use in making plant-bed soil at the close of the plant-growing season.

A more permanent method of constructing a manure-heated hotbed, one which will require the use of a relatively small amount of manure, is to dig a pit 6½ or 7 feet in width, from 14 to 30 inches in depth according to the severity of the climate, and of any desired length, the length usually being determined by the number of standard 3- by 6-foot sash that are to be used as a covering. The pit should be laid off with a line attached to stakes, as shown in figure 1, and then dug to the desired depth. It should then be lined with planks, as shown in figure 2, or with more permanent walls of brick, cement blocks, poured concrete, or some other material. The walls may extend aboveground to the desired height, and the sash rest directly upon them; or a framework of boards, 20 to 24 inches high at the back or north side and 10 to 12 inches high at the front or south side, may rest upon walls that come only to the ground level. If permanence is desired, the beds should be constructed entirely of the more durable materials with only such wood materials as are necessary to properly fit the sash tightly to the walls. In some cases crosspieces are provided upon which the sash rest, and this is a decided advantage for drawing down the sash for ventilation. An additional advantage is gained by having separation or guide stops between each sash so that there will be no danger of the sash slipping off the supporting members. The ends of the bed are cut on a slope to conform to the pitch or slope of the sash.

Manure for use in hotbeds should consist of a good grade of straw-bedded horse or mule manure; this should be hauled direct from the stable and should not be allowed to remain in piles where it will ferment and lose its heating qualities. The method of preparing and placing the manure in the pit of the hotbed is also of considerable importance. As it is hauled from the stable it should be placed

FIGURE 1.—Laying off and starting to dig a pit-type manure-heated hotbed.

FIGURE 2.—Pit hotbed with pit dug and framework of boards in place ready for manure to be forked into the bed.

in broad, flat piles alongside the hotbed, to remain 2 or 3 days, until it begins to heat; it should then be turned or forked over so as to secure uniform composition and heating. In case the manure is a trifle dry and shows a tendency to firefang or burn, a little water should be added as it is being turned. After 4 or 5 days, or as soon as the manure has begun to heat uniformly, it should be forked into the hotbed, care being taken to shake out all lumps and to spread the manure evenly in the bed. Figure 3 illustrates the proper method of trampling the manure as each layer is added. In case the manure is dry at the time it is being forked into the hotbed, a little water should again be added, but too much water may delay the heating.

The depth of the manure in the hotbed will depend on the outside temperatures. In localities where the temperature does not go below

FIGURE 3.—Trampling manure in pit of hotbed.

12° F. during the plant-growing period, a layer of manure 12 to 15 inches thick will be sufficient, provided the bed is well banked on the outside and some form of covering is used over the sash during periods of low temperature. The depth of the layer should be increased 1 inch for each degree of lowered temperature, about 24 to 28 inches of manure being used under conditions of 0° temperature. Following the placing of the manure in the bed, about 5 or 6 inches of screened garden loam should be spread evenly over the manure, and the sash put on to retain the heat. If sweetpotato plants are to be grown in the bed, clean sand should be used instead of the garden loam.

Figure 4 shows a small hotbed completed and the sash in place.

Cornstalks taken from the feed lot after the cattle have stripped the blades and husks from them have been found to be a good substitute for manure as a source of heat for hotbeds. The cornstalks are run through a silage cutter, then moistened and packed in the pit of the hotbed in exactly the same manner as manure. In the hotbed they go through a heating or fermentation process resembling that which takes place in a silo, and this results in the formation of enough heat to keep the plant bed warm over a period of 1 to 2 months. The labor involved in gathering the cornstalks from the feed lot and cutting them is largely offset by their disposal and conversion into readily available compost by the end of the plant-growing season. Where large quantities of cornstalks are to be used for hotbed heating the cutter should be placed alongside the beds and the chopped material blown directly into the beds. Where the

FIGURE 4.—The completed pit hotbed with sash in place.

quantity of manure for hotbed heating is limited, its volume and effectiveness can be increased by the addition of chopped or shredded corn fodder.

When a manure-heated bed is first made it is likely to heat very rapidly; the temperature may run into the 90's, or even above 100° F. This is too much heat, and the sowing of the seed should be delayed until the temperature falls to about 85° or lower. It is not safe to judge the temperature of the soil by feeling it. A thermometer should be used, its bulb buried in the soil to about the depth to which the seeds are planted. If at least 5 inches of sifted soil is placed over the manure in the bed, this soil will have a tendency to take up the heat given off by the manure, but it may be necessary to control the temperature by ventilation. Later, as the temperature of the manure in the bed declines, it may be necessary to bank more manure around the outside of the bed to maintain a proper temperature. If extra manure is not available, the outside of the bed should be securely banked with earth, marsh hay, straw, pine needles, or some other good insulating material.

FUEL-HEATED BEDS

Fuel-heated beds of various types are now largely replacing manure-heated beds, especially in sections where fuel is reasonably cheap, and where the manure supply is limited. The most common type of fuel-heated bed consists of a wood-burning furnace with one or more brick or tile smoke flues running underneath a floor upon which the soil is placed. Formerly, the fuel used in heating these beds consisted mainly of stumps and rough wood obtained when the land was cleared, but recently a type of furnace adapted to burning coke and hard coal is sometimes used. The present trend, however, is toward the pipe-heated bed in which hot water is employed as the medium of heat transmission. Where steam can be supplied at a constant but low pressure from a large or centralized boiler, as, for example, from a factory boiler, it may be used for heating hotbeds during the plant-growing season, but steam heat is a little too intense and not so easy to control as hot-water heat. Where steam is being used on a fairly large scale for heating plant beds the adoption of the vapor system will largely overcome the objection to steam. Steam heat does not require such large piping as hot-water heat, and sudden changes in temperature can be met to better advantage than with hot-water heat.

FLUE-HEATED BEDS

The truck growers of New Jersey and of the Eastern Shore, including Delaware and parts of Maryland and Virginia, use flue-heated beds very largely for starting early plants, especially tomatoes, peppers, and sweetpotatoes. These beds may be located on level ground, but oftener a location having a slight rise is selected. A pit about 18 inches deep, 8 to 12 feet wide, and 50 to 60 feet long is excavated, and the sides and ends are provided with plank, brick, or concrete walls extending 8 inches to a foot above the natural level of the soil. Frequently the pit is simply lined with boards nailed to stakes driven into the ground. In that case the boards extend about 12 inches aboveground to form the sides of the bed. A brick or stone furnace is built in a pit at the lower end of the bed, but outside the bed proper. A flue consisting of 6-inch or 8-inch round tile is connected with the furnace. Usually this flue is carried the full length of the bed and fitted with an elbow, and 3 or 4 joints of pipe are placed upright to form a chimney. In some cases two flues connected with the furnace are carried about half the length of the bed, and the smoke is discharged into the space under the floor of the bed, from which it eventually finds its way to a chimney at the end of the bed. The floor consists of planks laid on cross timbers which rest on the walls or on stone pillars at the sides.

The covering for these beds sometimes consists of marsh hay, but often it consists of heavy muslin or light canvas sewed together in a large sheet of sufficient size to cover the whole bed. A ridgepole is placed the full length through the center of the bed, and is supported on uprights about 2½ feet above the floor of the bed. Rafters or 1- by 3-inch or 1- by 4-inch strips are then fastened to the ridge and the sides of the bed every 3 or 4 feet to support the cover. At the sides of the bed the cover is fastened to long wooden strips on which it can be rolled up for ventilation or for watering. A bed of this type with marsh hay as a covering for the plants is shown in figure 5.

In some localities new railroad ties that have been rejected by the inspectors on account of some defect are used as supporting timbers

FIGURE 5.—A flue-heated plant bed having two flues or smoke ducts running the full length under the floor of the bed. Marsh hay is used as a covering for the bed.

for the floors of flue-heated beds. In that case the beds are made 8½ feet wide to conform to the length of the crossties. After the pit is dug, stone or brick pillars are built at intervals of 4 feet along the sides, and the crossties are laid with their ends resting on these stone or brick pillars. A floor of 2-inch planks is then laid upon the crossties; planks are placed on edge and are fastened to stakes to form the sides. In some cases brick or stone walls are used for the sides, and old boiler tubes or junk-yard pipe is let into the walls to form the cross supports. Old roofing tin, parts of old automobile bodies, or any discarded sheet metal may be used as flooring for these beds. The metal flooring and supports are strictly fireproof. However, there is little danger of fire with the wooden floors because of the low degree of heat maintained.

Instead of building a furnace of brick or stone, many growers cut one end out of an old 50-gallon steel oil barrel, and cut a hole in the opposite end large enough to admit the end of a 6-inch tile. The barrel is then buried on its side in a pit at one end of the bed, and a 6-inch tile is run from the opening of the barrel the full length of the bed under the floor, terminating in a chimney at the farther end of the bed. This chimney often consists of a wooden box which is carried 3 to 5 feet above the surface of the ground. Chunks of wood about 18 inches in length and 6 to 10 inches in diameter are used as fuel, and green sawdust is frequently placed on top of the wood in the furnace in order to give a slow-burning or smoldering fire. According to statements of growers, 1 cord of wood is sufficient to fire a bed of this character during a plant-growing season, and the fires require attention but twice in 24 hours. A piece of sheet iron held in place by an iron bar is used as a front door

FIGURE 6.—Type of flue- or stove-heated bed used by growers in southern New Jersey for starting early eggplant, tomato, and pepper plants.

for the furnace. When an extremely slow fire is desired, a piece of tile or a flat stone is laid partly over the chimney.

About 8 inches of good soil is placed on the floor of the bed in which the plants are to be grown, or, in the case of sweetpotatoes, sand is used. A bed of this type is shown in figure 5. Where sweetpotatoes are started in such beds, marsh hay is used almost exclusively as a covering, about 3 or 4 inches of the hay being spread loosely over the surface of the bed and the sweetpotato plants simply allowed to grow up through it. After the plants are well started, the hay is carefully removed with forks and rakes.

New Jersey growers frequently use a plant-growing bed of the type illustrated in figure 6. These beds or plant houses are constructed with a furnace pit and a smoke flue running from the furnace at the one end to a chimney at the other end. As a rule, the dimensions of these houses are 12 or 14 feet by 50 to 60 feet, with solid side beds and a walk through the center. Doors are provided at each end for convenience, and the covering consists of a framework on which hotbed sash rest. In the center of the bed and over the walk, the roof is constructed of boards that are covered with roofing paper or with tin. The sash are so arranged that they slip under the roofing at the top and can be either slid down or raised for ventilation. This type of bed or plant house has the advantage that the work of sowing seeds and transplanting can be done under cover during bad weather. During the summer and fall when the bed is not in use, the sash are removed and stored under shelter. In some cases the furnace and flues are omitted, but a stove is installed at one end, with a stovepipe running the full length of the house to supply the necessary heat. Where wood is plentiful, wood-burning stoves of the airtight type are used; where it is not to be had at a low cost, hard-coal stoves are employed on account of the uniformity of heating and the small amount of care required. In many cases these beds are being replaced by simple but effective greenhouses.

PIPE-HEATED BEDS

Another type of fuel-heated bed that is gaining popularity is constructed on level or nearly level ground with concrete side walls 12 to 18 inches high and lines of steam or hot-water pipes buried in the soil. Heat is obtained from a boiler located either in a pit at one end of the bed or in the basement of a service building nearby. In New Jersey, especially on farms where poultry is kept in connection with vegetable growing, the heater is placed under the workroom or tool room and supplies heat for both the hotbeds and the brooding houses. The heating pipes are usually laid lengthwise of the bed with the lines of piping 12 to 18 inches apart and at about the original soil level. The pipes should have a uniform fall of at least 6 inches in the length of a 60-foot bed, and should rest on solid earth or on bricks placed every 3 or 4 feet to prevent their settling and forming air pockets. Soil is filled in over the pipes to within about 6 inches of the top of the concrete walls, the pipes thus being 12 to 14 inches below the surface of the soil in the bed. A feed pipe is sometimes carried from the boiler to the far end of the bed, either along the ridge or on the side of the bed. It is there divided to supply the return pipes which are buried in the ground. More frequently, however, half of the pipes are used as flows and the other half as returns, the flows being elevated about 6 inches above the returns at the end of the bed next to the heater. Where this plan is followed, it is essential that the beds be located on a comparatively level piece of ground to obtain a uniform grade of the pipes both leaving and returning to the heater. Beds of this character are especially adapted for starting sweetpotato plants, and for peppers and eggplants which require an abundance of bottom heat. Figure 7 shows a cross section of a bed of this type.

Pipe-heated beds are also constructed with walls like ordinary 6-foot wood-frame or concrete hotbeds, but with the pipes arranged around the interior of the bed above the soil, the flow pipe being at the back or high side, and the return pipe at the low side and supported by pipe hangers or wires to the crossbars on which the sash rest. This type of bed gives good results where bottom heat is not required and where it is desired to grow stock plants somewhat slowly with merely enough heat to safeguard against low temperatures that would seriously check growth. Early plants of cabbage, cauliflower, lettuce, celery, and tomatoes can be grown to advantage

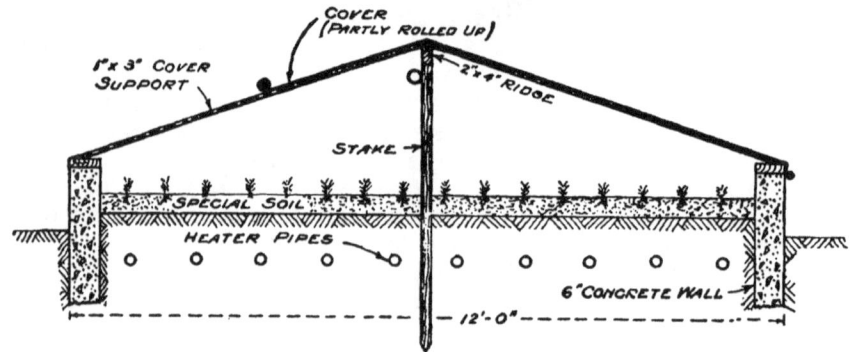

FIGURE 7.—Cross section of bed with heater pipes buried in the soil, the heat being supplied from a boiler.

in beds of this character. Figure 8 shows a cross section of this form of bed.

ELECTRIC HEATING OF BEDS AND PLANT HOUSES

For many years electricity has been used as a source of heat for plant-growing structures in Norway, Sweden, and other sections of northern Europe where water power has been extensively developed and electric energy is comparatively cheap. Experiments in this

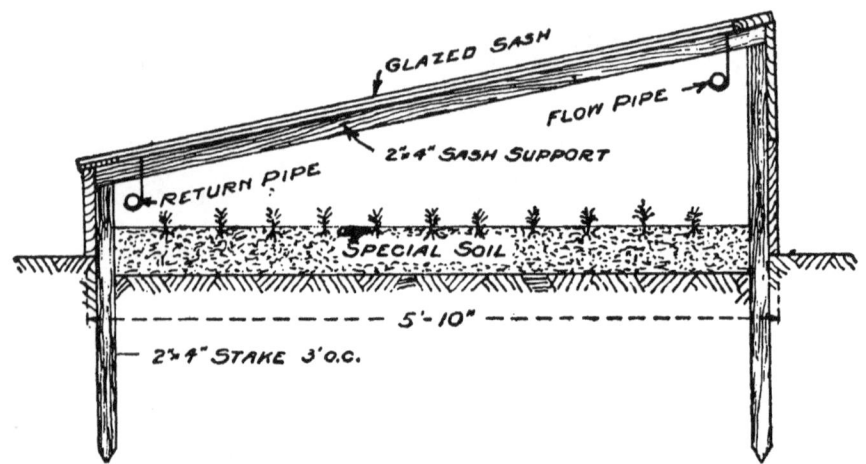

FIGURE 8.—Cross section of plant bed with two lines of heater pipes suspended from sash-support bars. For steam or hot-water heat.

country, especially those conducted by the State college and experiment station workers in certain States, have shown that under favorable conditions, electric current may be effectively and economically employed for heating outdoor plant beds and indoor propagating and seed-sprouting beds.[1] The first cost of installation, and the securing of suitable heating elements, together with the relative cost of electric energy as compared with manure and other sources of heat for plant beds, have been the limiting factors in the adoption of this form of heating.

This system has been found well adapted for heating propagating beds and small beds in which seeds are started. Figure 9 shows a bed of this character with the heater cable laid in the form of a coil in the bottom of the bed and partly covered with sand. The thermostat is also embedded in the sand and connected with the switch box and the feed wires at the end of the bed. The desired temperature may be easily maintained, but the main point is to have the bed well insulated to conserve the heat. One of the advantages of this form of heating for a seed or propagating bed is the uniformity at

FIGURE 9.—Electrically heated propagating bed showing heater cable in place before the bed was completely filled with sand or soil.

which the temperature may be maintained. The temperature can be regulated by simply turning the thermostat knob one way or the other, and when once regulated, the control is automatic.

Various types of heating units have been developed, the earlier types consisting of an open framework of wood or metal across which heating elements were stretched on insulators. These units were usually of the proper size and capacity for heating a 1-sash bed, 3 by 6 feet, and the frames carrying the heating elements were mounted in an enclosure underneath the floor of the bed. Later types of heating elements are insulated and enclosed in lead or copper cables that

---

[1] Wash. Agr. Expt. Sta. Bull. 219, Manure and Electric Hotbeds; Mo. Agr. Expt. Sta. Bull. 304, Electric Hotbeds; Idaho Agr. Expt. Sta. Circ. 68, Electric Soil and Hotbed Heating; Oreg. Agr. Expt. Sta. Bull. 307, Electric Hotbeds and Propagating Beds; Minn. Agr. Expt. Sta. Bull. 289, Methods of Supplying Electric Heat to Hotbeds; and National Rural Electric Project Repts. 5 and 6, Md. Agr. Expt. Sta., College Park, Md.

may be buried in the soil. These cables are made in various lengths, 60 feet being the length best adapted for use with the ordinary service current of 110 volts. One 60-foot cable is required for a 2-sash or 6- by 6-foot bed, and two 60-foot cables for a 4-sash or 12-foot bed where relatively high temperatures are desired. For a very moderate heat one 60-foot cable will be sufficient for a 4-sash bed 6 by 12 feet. Each 60-foot cable will carry an electrical load of approximately 403 watts, or about the amount of current required to operate ten 40-watt electric-light bulbs. The arrangement of the cables in the bed is shown in figure 10.

Heat conservation is the keynote in handling electrically heated plant beds. The sides and ends of the beds should be tight, and, in addition, should be banked to the top with earth or some material to conserve heat. The sash should fit snugly, and, if needed to make the joints tight, strips of felt or rubber should be tacked to the

FIGURE 10.—Arrangement of heater in an ordinary 6- by 12-foot hotbed.

edges of the bed on which the sash rest. The glass should be well bedded in putty, and should lap one-fourth inch at the joints. In addition to the glass, the beds should be covered with straw or felt hotbed mats during cold nights. In case of extremely cold weather the sash may be doubled by placing one sash on top of another, and banking the edges of the sash with straw, pine needles, or with leaves held in place by means of boards.

Electrically heated plant beds have a decided operating advantage over the ordinary manure- and fuel-heated beds in that the amount of heat can be automatically controlled by the use of thermostats or regulators, thus avoiding extremes. In the case of manure-heated beds the temperature usually runs too high at first, then declines rapidly, and finally becomes completely exhausted. Another advantage over manure heating is that the electric heating is free from odors or gases, and no steam or excessive moisture is formed. Electrically heated beds require very little attention to ventilation, except on very bright days when the heat of the sun is sufficient to raise the temperature of the bed above the maximum for the best plant growth. Where electric current can be obtained at a power rate the cost of heating plant beds compares favorably with manure heating at present prices of manure. When once the electric system is installed very little labor is required to renew the surface soil and get the beds in shape for planting. The copper and lead cables are highly resistant to corrosion, and, unless injured by tools, should last for years. Because of the uniform control of temperature, it is reasonable to expect that better plants can be grown with electric heat than with manure heat. Plants grown in electrically heated beds usually require a little more attention to watering than those grown in manure-heated beds.

FIGURE 11.—Electrically heated plant bed with heater cables buried in soil and running the full length of the bed.

One firm in New Jersey has adopted electricity as the main source of heat for plant beds and small greenhouses in which early plants are grown. Figure 11 shows one of these beds in which the electric heating elements run the full length of the bed and are buried in the soil. Sash are used as a covering for this bed, and the soil temperature is controlled by an automatic thermostat. This firm is operating a number of sash-covered plant houses of the type shown in figure 12 which are electrically heated. Both the underground and overhead systems of heating are being employed in these houses to determine which gives the better results. Recently in a test of indirect electric heating, fans were used to drive the air over the heating elements and distribute it to the various parts of the house. This type of installation simplifies construction problems and gives a better circulation of heat than the old method of stringing the heating elements through the open spaces in the house. The action of the fans tends to provide better ventilation.

CONSTRUCTION OF COLDFRAMES

The construction of coldframes is practically the same as that of hotbeds, except that no provision is made for heating them artificially. Coldframes consisting of a framework of boards from 18 to 24 inches in height at the back or north side, and 8 to 12 inches at the front or south side, are generally built directly on top of the ground (figs. 13 and 14). Sometimes these beds are made in units of five sash each, with sloping ends and crosspieces to support the sash, but oftener they consist of two lines of boards fastened to stakes driven into the ground and without crosspieces, the sash resting on top of the edges of the boards forming the front and back of the bed. Frames of this character are used for the growing and hardening of early

FIGURE 12.—An electrically heated plant bed in which both air and soil heating are employed.

plants, the boards and sash being removed and stored as soon as the plant-growing season is over. This type of coldframe is also used extensively along the Atlantic coast for the growing to maturity of such crops as lettuce, beets, carrots, parsley, and cucumbers.[2] Figure 15 shows a 1-acre frame yard near Portsmouth, Va. Parsley was being grown in these frames when the picture was taken.

COVERINGS FOR HOTBEDS AND COLDFRAMES

Coverings for both hotbeds and coldframes consist of standard hotbed sash, various kinds of glass substitutes, and cloth coverings such as muslin or light canvas. In some instances, a covering of straw or marsh hay is placed directly on the soil in the beds and is removed after the plants appear above ground, or the plants may be allowed to grow up through it, as is sometimes done in starting

---

[2] Farmers' Bulletin 1563, Cucumber Growing, gives information on the use of coldframes for growing early cucumbers.

FIGURE 13.—Coldframe, constructed of boards nailed to stakes driven into the ground, ready for sash or cloth cover.

FIGURE 14.—Coldframe with sash covering in place.

sweetpotato plants. The most satisfactory covering for hotbeds and coldframes in the northern sections is glazed hotbed sash, supplemented by hotbed mats, board shutters, slat screens, and hay or pine straw. To the southward, where the covering can be left off the greater part of the time, a cloth covering, especially heavy unbleached muslin, has been found to give good results.

GLAZED-SASH COVERINGS

Standard hotbed sash are 3 feet wide, 6 feet long, and 1⅜ or 1¾ inches thick, and carry three rows of 10-inch glass. A reinforcing rod of ⅜-inch iron, or a strip of wood or metal, is placed across the center of each sash to strengthen it. These sash, made of clear gulf cypress, white pine, or California redwood, are kept in stock by dealers in greenhouse supplies and can be furnished unglazed and unpainted, unglazed and painted with 2 coats, or

FIGURE 15.—One-acre frame yard near Portsmouth, Va., where a crop of parsley is being grown. Note the method of ventilating.

fully glazed with double-strength glass and painted with 2 or 3 coats of white-lead paint, according to the desire of the purchaser. Sash 4 feet in width and 7 to 9 feet in length can be secured on special order. The prices of hotbed sash vary according to the lumber market and the cost of labor and materials going into their construction.

Experience has shown that if the sash are kept well painted and are stored under cover when they are not in use, they will last from 10 to 20 years or even longer. The sash should be given a first or priming coat consisting of white lead and pure raw linseed oil, to which should be added enough turpentine to cause the paint to penetrate the wood. The second coat, which should be applied before glazing, should contain a little Japan drier to cause the paint to dry readily. As a rule it will pay to give the sash a third or finish coat of paint after glazing. Figure 16 shows the upper side of a standard 3- by 6-foot hotbed sash fully glazed and painted and ready to place on the hotbed.

Hotbed sash should be glazed with fresh or plastic putty that will spread evenly on the sash bars, or with one of the prepared glazing compounds that are applied with a putty gun. The glass should be firmly embedded in the putty, the lights overlapping one-eighth to one-fourth of an inch, beginning at the bottom of the sash. Each light of glass should be fastened with 4 zinc glazing sprigs, 2 of these being driven on top of the glass about an inch from its lower edge and 2 directly below the edge of the glass to hold it from slipping toward the lower end of the sash. Cut a piece of glass to fill the remaining space at the top of the course, being sure that it is forced well up into the groove, previously filled with soft putty, at the top of the sash. Trim off all surplus putty above and below the glass and do not putty above the glass as in glazing an ordinary window.

FIGURE 16.—Top view of a standard 3- by 6-foot hotbed sash, fully glazed, painted, and ready to place on the hotbed.

Hotbed sash, in which the sash bars are made with grooves into which the glass can be slipped without the use of putty, are commonly used in sections having a mild climate. As a rule 6- by 8-inch single-strength glass is used, the glass being pushed in from the lower end of the sash and the lights butted together. This type of glazing does not give as warm a covering for the beds as the regular puttied and lapped glass and is subject to greater dripping of rainwater upon the plant beds. The glazing of this type of sash is a very simple matter, and in case of a light of glass becoming broken a new light can simply be slipped in at the bottom and the whole line of glass shoved up to close the opening.

Formerly, all window glass, except plate glass, had a slight bow or curve but flat glass is now used almost exclusively. Although it is of little importance which side of the old-type curved glass is placed upward, it should all be laid one way. Nearly all gardeners, however, place it with the bow or hump side uppermost. Double-strength glass is preferable to single-strength, as it is less subject to breakage in handling. Grade B glass is most commonly used for glazing hotbed sash, but should be free from blisters.

CLOTH COVERINGS

In the southern sections, where the climate is mild and cloth coverings are largely used, the beds are usually constructed 12 to 14 feet in width and with a ridgepole supported on stakes about 30 inches high through the center of the bed. The muslin or light canvas used for the cover is sewed together in a large sheet and is fastened to the ridgepole by tacking thin strips of wood such as plaster lath or lattice strips on top of the sheet and to the ridgepole. The edges of the sheet are generally fastened to strips of wood running the full

FIGURE 17.—Cloth-covered tomato-plant bed in eastern Texas. The plant beds are located directly in the field where the tomato crop is to be grown for convenience in transferring plants from the bed to the open ground.

length at each side of the bed, and so arranged that the sheet can be rolled up on them (fig. 17).

Rafters consisting of $7/8$- by 3-inch or $7/8$- by 4-inch strips are nailed to the ridgepole and to the sides of the bed at intervals of 3 or 4 feet to support the cloth; the cloth is carried on these rafters when it is rolled up for ventilation. At the ends of the bed the cloth is fastened by loops of string hooked over nails. Marsh hay, light straw, or pine straw is often spread over the cloth during periods of cold weather. Beds containing tender plants, such as tomatoes, are frequently protected successfully for short periods with a temperature of 20° F. by this method of covering.

There are processes for treating cotton sheeting to make it waterproof and to preserve it, but, as a rule, a good grade of unbleached muslin without treatment is satisfactory. Preservatives may add to the life of the covering material, but if the muslin is taken off the plant beds promptly when the plant-growing season is over, rolled while dry, and stored in a dry place, it will last for several years.

Linseed oil, or any paint containing linseed or other drying oils, should not be used for waterproofing plant-bed covers as the oil paints rot the fabric and cause it to crack and break. A mixture consisting of 2 to 3 pounds of melted paraffin, one-half pound of melted beeswax, and 1 gallon of benzine applied to the cloth either as a spray or with a brush will act as a filler to make the fabric waterproof and at the same time preserve it. There are on the market preparations used for waterproofing tents and canvas generally which can be used for making ordinary heavy unbleached muslin both waterproof and windproof.[3]

SUBSTITUTES FOR GLASS AND CLOTH

Numerous substitutes for glass and cloth as coverings for hotbeds and coldframes are on the market, but many unwarranted claims are made concerning the effect of some substitutes on plant growth. In 1928 and 1929 the Ohio Agricultural Experiment Station showed that while a good grade of clear glass transmits over 95 percent of the total light, certain substitutes transmitted as little as 25 percent and none of those tested more than 60 percent. Although these particular substitutes transmitted only 25 to 60 percent of the total light, they did transmit an appreciable percentage of ultra-violet light. In ordinary plant-growing operations, the transmission of ultra-violet light is of no recognizable benefit, but the decreased transmission of total light is a definite disadvantage. The Ohio tests showed that better plants were grown under plain glass than could be grown under any of the substitutes tried. The Connecticut Agricultural Experiment Station has found certain clear cellulose films to be good glass substitutes when properly handled.

CARE OF HOTBEDS AND COLDFRAMES

Regardless of the method of securing heat, the ventilation, watering, and general care of the hotbed or coldframe are of vital importance. The temperature of a manure-heated bed will usually run fairly high at first, and planting should be deferred until the temperature begins to decrease. The only safe procedure is to bury a thermometer bulb in the soil of the bed and delay planting until the temperature reading is 80° F., or lower. A soil temperature of about 70° or 72° is about right for nearly all early plants. However, it will be safe to plant the seeds when the temperature is slightly below 80°, for it will gradually decline as the fermentation of the manure diminishes. With bottom heat, such as is furnished by fermenting manure or pipes buried in the soil, the germination and early growth of the plants will be very rapid, and unless frequent attention is given to ventilation, the plants are certain to make a soft growth. In the manure-heated bed there is a constant supply of extra heat which can be controlled only by ventilating the bed. With a pipe- or furnace-heated bed, and where electric current is used, the bottom heat can be controlled almost at will.

Different crops require different temperatures and treatment; the temperature that gives best results for starting peppers and egg-

---

[3] Farmers' Bulletin 1157, Waterproofing and Mildewproofing of Cotton Duck. Out of print. May be consulted in libraries.

plant, for example, would be too high for tomatoes and much too high for cabbage, cauliflower, and lettuce. The desirable temperatures at which to grow the plants will be discussed later under the various crops.

VENTILATION

In ventilating the hotbed or coldframe during windy weather, care must be taken to raise the sash or cloth covering on the side opposite from that from which the wind is blowing so as to avoid a direct draft upon the plants. In the sash-covered bed, this is accomplished by lifting the sash on either side, or at the bottom or top, as the direction of the wind may require. Small pieces of boards or blocks of wood with notches cut in them are usually employed to support the sash. In some cases wires are stretched lengthwise of the beds on top of the sash to prevent them from being blown off during storms.

Where cloth or muslin coverings are used, ventilation is obtained by rolling them up a part or all of the way to the ridge of the bed, as shown in figure 17, or by propping them up in places by means of short pieces of lath. Special protection is provided during short periods of extremely cold weather by covering the beds with hotbed mats or with a thin layer of straw or pine straw that must be removed when the weather clears and the temperature rises. The straw can be removed from the glass or cloth covers by first using a wooden rake and then a broom to complete the cleaning.

In order to secure the greatest possible benefit from the sunlight, the glass or whatever covering is used should be kept thoroughly clean. Dust settling on top of the glass will frequently cut out 25 to 30 percent of the light. For that reason the glass should be frequently cleaned with brooms or water from a hose. The best of plant-bed coverings exclude considerable light, and every precaution should be taken to keep this exclusion to a minimum.

Coldframes are managed in practically the same manner as hotbeds in respect to ventilation and protection from sudden changes in temperature. As a rule, somewhat lower temperatures are maintained in coldframes than in hotbeds, but they require close attention on extremely bright days and during changeable weather. Clouds temporarily obscuring the sun will frequently cause a lowering of the temperature in the frames of from 12° to 15° F. Toward the end of the plant-growing period the sash or cloth coverings may be kept partly open at all times and finally be removed altogether to adapt the plants to outside conditions.

WATERING

Early in the season, extreme care is necessary in watering hotbeds and coldframes, because excessive watering is almost certain to cause damping-off of the plants. More water is required during bright, windy weather than when it is calm or cloudy. Watering should be done only at times when the beds may be safely opened without chilling the plants. Losses from damping-off can be largely prevented by careful watering and close attention to ventilation. Overheating of the beds is disastrous and results in the production of poor plants. Sufficient ventilation, especially toward the end of the period that the plants remain in the beds, with a somewhat sparing application of water, will produce plants that will withstand transplanting to the field with few losses.

The process of "hardening", as applied to plants grown under cover, consists of gradually tempering them to open-air conditions by checking their growth, but taking care to avoid stunting injury. Certain plants, especially eggplants, should be checked but slightly, if at all, for if their stems become tough and woody they are practically worthless for planting. Tomato plants will stand considerable checking but are injured if the process goes too far. Light watering usually aids in the tempering process; however, enough water must be applied at all times to prevent wilting. Excessive ventilation and windy weather are always accompanied by high evaporation and make extra care and more frequent watering necessary.

Plants grown to marketable stage in hotbeds and coldframes require somewhat different handling as to temperature and watering than do those that are to be transplanted to the open ground. With those that remain in the beds the hardening process is not used, and the plants are kept growing uniformly and usually as rapidly as possible without producing a soft growth. This is accomplished by careful regulation of the temperature and by the application of water in quantities that will maintain an optimum growth condition in the soil. In the growing of plants for transplanting, a period of relatively high temperature at first, followed by a declining temperature and the application of practically no artificial heat toward the end of the period, is ideal. In the case of the crop that is matured in the beds, the most satisfactory results are obtained with a continuous mild heat without excessive changes in temperature.

GROWING EARLY PLANTS

Plants that are normally grown under protection for early transplanting to the garden and truck fields may be classified into two general groups according to their temperature requirements. In the first group are those requiring a relatively low temperature; and in the second group are those requiring a somewhat higher temperature. Among the most important of the lower temperature plants frequently started indoors and transplanted are lettuce, cabbage, cauliflower, and broccoli. The crops requiring a somewhat higher temperature include tomatoes, peppers, eggplants, muskmelons, summer squashes, celery, and cucumbers. There are, however, within these groups certain very important crop-requirement differences that are briefly discussed in the following paragraphs.

TOMATOES

Tomato seed germinates readily at a soil temperature between 68° and 75° F., but when the seedlings appear aboveground the temperature should be lowered slightly to prevent weak and spindling plants. The time required for germination of tomato seed depends to some degree upon the viability of the seed itself, but good seed will germinate in 3 to 5 days at a temperature of 72° to 75° and in 5 to 8 days at temperatures from 65° to 70°. A soil temperature of about 62°

to 65°, with plenty of light and moderate watering, will usually produce good stocky seedlings, but the air temperatures should not be allowed to go much above 70° at any time. Plants grown in this manner will usually be ready for transplanting from the seed-trays or from the hotbed to the coldframe in 14 to 20 days after the seed is sown. If the seed is sown rather thinly and the plants do not crowd in the seedbed nothing is to be gained by extra-early transplanting to the coldframe. Plenty of ventilation and care in watering will generally obviate losses of the plants from the disease known as damping-off.

Early-tomato growers of eastern Texas and Mississippi sow the seed in hotbeds and transplant the seedlings to cloth-covered coldframes located directly in the field where the crop is to be grown. As a rule one plant bed measuring about 12 by 60 feet (fig. 17) is provided for each acre of tomatoes to be planted.[4]

The plants are spaced about 4 inches apart in each direction in the coldframe, and when the time comes for setting them in the field a knife or a trowel is run between the plants in each direction and they are lifted and transported to the field with blocks of earth about their roots.

In sections where tomatoes are grown largely for the cannery, the seed is sown rather thinly in the seedbeds, and after 4 to 6 weeks, or when the plants attain a height of 4 to 6 inches, they are moved directly to the fields. This method involves less labor than transplanting the plants from the seedbed to coldframes and later to the field, but does not give as desirable plants for early setting.

PEPPERS

Pepper seed is rather slow to germinate, usually requiring from 12 to 15 days at a soil temperature of 70° to 75°. Following germination the soil temperature should be lowered to 65°, or not over 68°, in order to produce stocky plants. The air temperature following germination should be kept between 65° and 75°. The same precautions as to watering and ventilation should be taken with peppers as with tomatoes. The danger of damping-off can be largely eliminated by avoiding excessive watering and at the same time providing plenty of ventilation. The pepper seedlings will be ready for transplanting from the hotbed to the coldframe in 24 to 30 days after the seed is sown. Under the best conditions and where the seed germinates in a relatively short time the plants may be ready for this transplanting in 18 to 20 days after seeding. After being transplanted, the pepper plants should be carefully watched, and when first transplanted they should be partially shaded to prevent wilting. Following this the temperature of the coldframe should be between 70° and 75° during the daytime and not lower than 60° at night. In removing the pepper plants from the coldframe to the garden or field, they are blocked and a cube of soil carried with them to their permanent location.

EGGPLANTS

The eggplant is one of the most difficult vegetables to handle, especially during its early stages. The seed germinates somewhat

---

[4] See Farmers' Bulletin 1338, Tomatoes as a Truck Crop.

slowly even at a soil temperature slightly above 70° F. Extreme care must be taken to keep the eggplant seedlings growing uniformly from the very start, for if the plants become checked and the stems hardened or woody, they are considered practically worthless for planting in the field or garden. As a rule the seedlings will be ready to transplant from the hotbed to a well-protected or warm coldframe in about 3 or 4 weeks after the seed is sown. In the coldframe the plants should be set at least 5 inches apart in each direction in a soil that is well fertilized and that contains an abundance of well-rotted, screened manure. At no time should the plants be subjected to strong drafts of cold air or to low temperatures. Excessive watering of the plants both in the hotbed and in the coldframe must be avoided. On the other hand, the soil in which the plants are growing should never be allowed to become too dry, as this is certain to result in a stunting of the growth of the plants. In moving the plants from the bed to the field they are blocked, and a large cube of earth is carried with them. The soil about their roots should be fairly well watered a few hours before the plants are to be lifted. Throughout the handling of the plants, extreme care must be taken as otherwise they will not grow in a satisfactory manner in the field, regardless of the attention that is given them after they are set out.

SUMMER SQUASHES

Under most conditions the seed of summer squashes is planted directly in the hills where the crop is to be grown. Where extreme earliness is desirable, however, the plants may be started in heated plant houses or in hotbeds, inverted pieces of sod, berry boxes, paper bands, or flowerpots being used for the purpose. The seed of squashes will germinate in about 2 days at a soil temperature of about 75° F. After the seeds have germinated, the temperature should be lowered somewhat in order to keep the plants short and stocky. Where squashes are started indoors it is customary to plant six or seven seeds in each container; then, when the seedlings are well established, thin them to three plants. After the seedlings have formed the first true leaf they can be moved to a well-protected coldframe, where the plants may be held at a temperature of 60° to 70° until time to set them in the garden or truck field. By starting the plants in hotbeds and coldframes, most of the difficulty with the striped and spotted cucumber beetles can be avoided. By this process the first of the crop can be ready to market from 1 to 2 weeks earlier than when the seed is planted in the open.

CUCUMBERS

The growers of early cucumbers in the Norfolk-Portsmouth, Va., district follow the practice of sowing their cucumber seed in specially heated beds with the soil temperature between 80° and 85° F. The seeds are sown fairly thick in rows, and, as a rule, the seedlings will appear above ground within 30 to 36 hours. In approximately 72 hours after sowing, the seedlings are ready to be lifted and placed in 5-inch flowerpots, 7 to 10 seedlings being planted in each pot. These pots are then placed in the bench of a greenhouse at a temperature of 70° to 75° during the day and not lower than 60° or 65°

at night, and the plants are carefully watered and ventilated for about 4 weeks, when they will have formed about 3 or 4 true leaves. During this period the plants are thinned to about 3 in each pot. They are then in proper condition for setting in outdoor frames.[5]

In moving the plants from the greenhouse to frames or to the fields the soil in the pots is given a fair watering, then the plants are carried direct to the field, where they are loosened from the pots and set in the ground with the ball of earth about their roots. Cucumbers may be grown in the hotbed in quart berry boxes, paper bands, or flowerpots, the seed being sown directly in the containers, which are filled with a good grade of sifted soil. The corners of the boxes should be slit with a knife and the boxes removed when the plants are set in the ground.

MUSKMELONS

Muskmelon seedlings are frequently started in hotbeds in the same manner as cucumbers; however, it is not customary to start the seed in a special heated seedbed and transplant the seedlings, although this can be done safely. The rule is to use pieces of inverted sod, berry boxes, or paper bands and plant 10 to 12 muskmelon seeds in each container. After the seedlings become established they are thinned first to about 5 and later to 3 plants to each hill. Muskmelons require practically the same temperature conditions as cucumbers, and the methods of handling the plants and transferring them to the field are practically the same as those given for cucumbers and squashes. The advantages of starting the muskmelons indoors are earliness of fruiting and less liability to injury from the striped cucumber beetle. It is desirable to give the plants one spraying in the plant bed with bordeaux mixture before they are moved to the field.

LETTUCE

Lettuce is one of the more important garden crops that thrive under a moderately low temperature. The seed is one of the few that does not germinate readily when it is strictly fresh, and it should not be planted during the fall of the year in which it is produced. When growing lettuce plants indoors the usual practice is to sow the seed in boxes or trays filled with a good grade of garden loam which has been thoroughly mixed and sifted. Generally the seed will germinate in 4 to 6 days, and the plants will be ready for transplanting in 12 to 15 days. The seedlings can be transplanted from the seed trays or the hotbed to the coldframe either in other trays or direct to the soil of the coldframe. As a rule, the plants are spaced about 3 inches in each direction so as to give them enough room to develop and allow for the transfer of a fair-sized block of soil around the roots of the plants when they are taken to the garden or the truck field. Lettuce seedlings are subject to damping-off in the seedbed, especially where the seed has been sown too thick. This difficulty can be avoided by thin seeding, careful watering, and plenty of ventilation, although the use of a mercury bichloride solution may be found advantageous in checking this disease.[6]

---

[5] For further information see Farmers' Bulletin 1563, Cucumber Growing.
[6] For further information see Farmers' Bulletin 1371, Diseases and Insects of Garden Vegetables, and Farmers' Bulletin 1609, Lettuce Growing.

CABBAGE AND BROCCOLI

Early plants of cabbage and broccoli are frequently started in hotbeds or in well-protected coldframes. About 4 or 5 weeks are required from the time of sowing the seed to produce good cabbage or broccoli plants for setting in the garden. Where the seed is sown in the hotbed it will be necessary to transplant the seedlings to a coldframe because the temperature of the hotbed is too high for the production of good stocky cabbage or broccoli plants. The soil temperature of the seedbed should not be above 70° F. After transplanting to the coldframe the air temperature should be maintained at about 65° to 70° during the day and 55° to 60° at night; however, a drop in temperature to perhaps 45° for a short period as a rule will not greatly injure these plants. Repeated chilling or carrying the plants at low temperatures for a period of 2 weeks or more may cause them to bolt to seed after they are set in the field or garden. In sections of the country where the climate is fairly warm during the early spring a hotbed for starting the early plants will not be necessary; the seed can be merely sown in a coldframe or in a flue-heated bed similar to those used for starting sweetpotatoes. Fairly thin seeding will produce better plants than overcrowding the seedlings. The same general methods given for cabbage should be followed in the production of broccoli plants.

CAULIFLOWER

Cauliflower plants are decidedly more delicate in their habits of growth than those of either cabbage or broccoli, and for that reason require more careful handling. The main point in the handling of cauliflower plants is to keep them growing and to prevent checking or stunting during the time they are in the plant bed. In case the stems of cauliflower become tough or woody this stunting affects their future growth and usually results in the formation of small and inferior heads of cauliflower; therefore, cauliflower plants require a little higher temperature and closer attention than those of cabbage or broccoli. They also require very careful watering, because drying out will affect their growth and will have a tendency to cause them to be tough and woody. Besides having a uniform temperature maintained and being given proper ventilation, cauliflower plants should be given plenty of space, and when they are transplanted from the seedbed to the coldframe or other space where they are to remain until they are planted in the field they should be well shaded for a day or two. In being moved from the hotbed or coldframe to the field or garden, cauliflower plants should not be pulled, as cabbage plants frequently are, but should be lifted with considerable soil adhering to their roots. In case the soil should be dry at the time the plants are set out, they should be given a good watering as they are set. If possible, a calm, cloudy, moist day should be selected for setting the cauliflower plants in the field or garden.

CELERY

Celery seed is slow in starting, and the seedbed must be carefully watched to prevent drying out. Seed stored in a dry place usually retains its vitality for 4 or 5 years, but where old seed is used it should be carefully tested in advance of planting time. Good, viable celery seed will germinate in 10 to 15 days at a soil temperature of about 63° to 68° F.; where the seed is sown directly in a hotbed the sowing should be delayed until the heat of the bed is well spent and the soil temperature has fallen below 70°. In the greenhouse a temperature varying between 60° and 70° is about right; where the seed is sown in flats a partially shaded location is desirable until the seedlings appear, after which full sunlight and a fair amount of ventilation should be provided.

In sections where muck or peat is available this material is largely used for starting celery plants. A seedbed consisting of 2 parts good garden loam, 1 part fine but sharp sand, and 1 part leafmold or old decayed compost thoroughly mixed and sifted through a screen having four meshes to the inch will give good results. Watering is very important to keep the seedbed properly moistened and ventilation to avoid overwatering and the development of the damping-off disease. Thin seeding will aid very materially in the prevention of this disease, but careful watering and plenty of ventilation are also essential.

A few growers still double transplant early celery plants. The main or late crop, however, is grown from seedlings that are started in spent hotbeds or in coldframes, or from outdoor plant beds.

Celery belongs to the group of garden vegetables that thrives under relatively cool conditions, but recent experiments have shown that prolonged periods of low temperature during the plant-growing period is largely responsible for celery bolting or shooting to seed prematurely. Under normal conditions celery is a biennial and produces its seed crop the second season, but under certain conditions the plants shoot to seed during the first season and fail to produce an edible crop.

It has been a common practice among the northern growers of early-crop celery to start the seedlings in a greenhouse and transfer them to coldframes. In some cases the plants are held in the greenhouse for several weeks and then transferred to the coldframe where they are hardened at temperatures below 60° F., usually between 40° and 50°. If this hardening period extends beyond 2 weeks at a temperature below 60° a large percentage of the crop is fairly certain to bolt to seed before it has reached a marketable stage. It is not necessary to use low temperatures for hardening the plants, as this can be accomplished by light watering. In case the plants are subjected to temperatures below 60° in order to harden them the treatment should be given for a week or 10 days only, and during that time water should be used sparingly. Celery plants grown in the open during the early part of the season may go to seed if relatively low temperatures prevail during the plant-growing period. High temperatures during June and July may, however, correct this difficulty.

For sale by the Superintendent of Documents, U. S. Government Printing Office
Washington 25, D. C. Price 10 cents